MAX
and the Diaper Fairy

Melissa L. Hart   Megan Stringfellow

ISBN 978-0-615-31269-9

www.maxandthediaperfairy.com

This book belongs to:

_____

This book is dedicated to my little angels,
Alex and Austin.

May you soar high to your fullest potential in this world
and always embrace the gift of imagination.

- Melissa L. Hart

MAX
and the Diaper Fairy

It was a sunny day, and Max was reading a book about sharing with his mommy.

"Do you know where we are going today?" asked his mommy. "Yes, we are going to the park," said Max. "And, I will see my friends!"

Max was a gentle little boy who loved to play with his friends.

"Today I play with the BIG kids," said Max.

"What makes them BIG kids?" asked his mommy.

"They don't wear diapers," he said.

Max was growing up so fast----BUT, he still wore diapers.

He knew he should use the potty. But for some reason, he did not want to.

One day Max shouted, "I am NOT going to use the potty!"

One night, the doorbell rang.

"Who is it, Daddy?" asked Max. "It looks like someone left a letter for you," he said.

"Open it, open it! " Max shouted.

Dear Max,
I am the Diaper Fairy and I have been watching you.

I visit little boys and girls who are ready to use the potty. I will bring you new and fun underwear, and my special Magic Fairy Dust.

I am coming to your house tomorrow night. Please put all of your unused diapers in a big bag, and I will give them to little babies in the world who really need them.

You are such a BIG boy.

I Love You,

The Diaper Fairy

Max was worried.

"She is going to take all of my diapers away!" he cried.

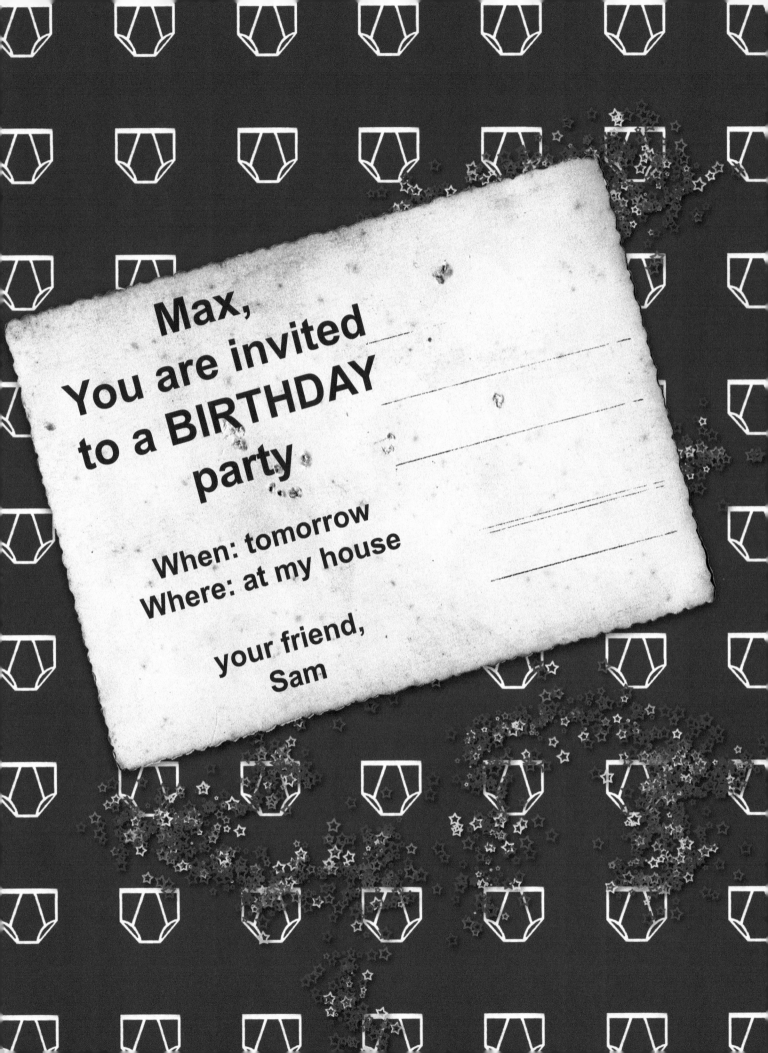

Max,
You are invited
to a BIRTHDAY
party

When: tomorrow
Where: at my house

your friend,
Sam

The next day, Max went to a birthday party with his BIG friends.

He ate his favorite cake and yummy ice cream, with a cherry on top!

He wondered if he could be like his friends and wear underwear.

Max and his mommy got all of his diapers and put them in a big bag for the Diaper Fairy. Max was a little sad.

He loved his diapers. But The Diaper Fairy was going to bring him special underwear and make him big and strong to use the potty.

Max closed his eyes and went to sleep. He began to dream about how his diapers would help little babies all over the world. They were so very thankful to have diapers.

"Hi Max, I am the Diaper Fairy."

Max was very quiet. His eyes grew bigger and bigger, as he looked at her.

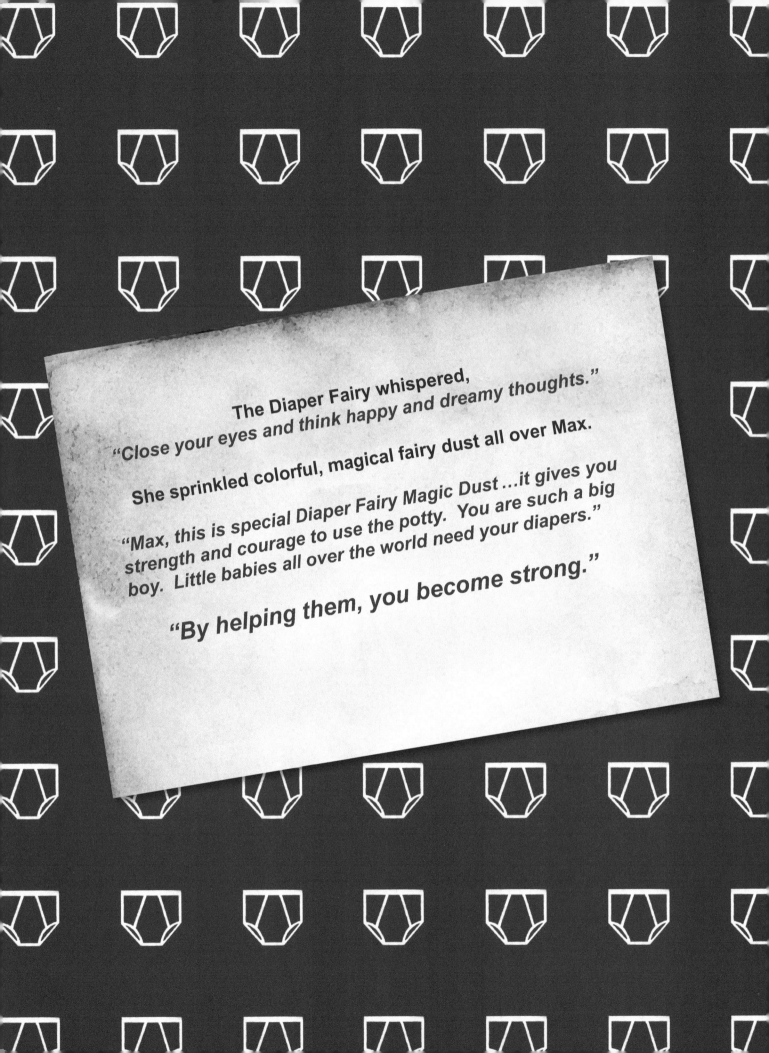

The Diaper Fairy whispered,
"Close your eyes and think happy and dreamy thoughts."

She sprinkled colorful, magical fairy dust all over Max.

"Max, this is special Diaper Fairy Magic Dust ...it gives you strength and courage to use the potty. You are such a big boy. Little babies all over the world need your diapers."

"By helping them, you become strong."

After she sprinkled the magic dust all over him, Max felt so BIG and STRONG—*LIKE HE COULD DO ANYTHING!*

The Diaper Fairy opened up her silver bag and gave Max a whole bunch of fun underwear.

As she went out the window, she whispered, *"You are such a BIG boy. I will be watching over you. Good-bye and sweet dreams!"*

The next day, Max went to play with his friends.

He is a BIG kid. He wore his new underwear and was just like his friends.

Everyone was so happy to see Max.

Max was so proud that he met the Diaper Fairy. He was glad that his diapers were going to little babies who really needed them.

He could not wait to start using the potty every day.

Max looked up to the sky and shouted:

"Thank you, Diaper Fairy! I LOVE YOU!"

Are _you_ a BIG kid?

Are _you_ ready to help little babies
in the world?

When is The Diaper Fairy coming
to see _you_?

The End

Information on Diaper Banks

Max and the Diaper Fairy is proud to join forces with The Diaper Bank of Southern AZ to help promote diaper donations across the nation. Known as the nation's FIRST Diaper Bank, The Diaper Bank of Southern AZ was founded in 1994 and has distributed over 6 million diapers.

Did you know that Food Stamps do not cover diapers? They never did. We know that people and families who need diapers probably need other social services as well, so the Diaper Bank provides diapers to existing organizations who work with people in need. A healthy change of diapers costs an average of $100 a month or more. This is a huge, sometimes out-of-reach, expense for low-income families and seniors on fixed incomes.

- *The likelihood of abuse increases when a baby is in a household facing the stresses of poverty, and increases even more when that baby is screaming and crying because their diaper is soiled.*

- *A parent who cannot afford diapers cannot leave their child at daycare, and therefore cannot work or go to school to improve their situation. Unbelievably, that single package of diapers can make that much of a difference in their lives.*

- *A disabled person who cannot afford incontinence supplies cannot work, cannot live independently. And the parents of a disabled child may never be relieved of the expense of diapering their child - even when the child is 8 or 13 or 22.*

To find a Diaper Bank in your area or to learn how you can start a diaper bank in your town, please visit *www.diaperbank.org* or *www.diaperbanksofamerica.org* for more information.

About The Author

As a mom of two very active boys, Melissa had spent 20 years in corporate America, juggling full time work and raising her children with her husband in Arizona. The concept of the Diaper Fairy was born in those hectic days—now over ten years ago—when her eldest refused to use the potty. The traditional approaches and numerous stories about potties were not working.

Over night, Melissa became the Diaper Fairy and helped her son make the magical transition in one day—thanks to a little Diaper Fairy Magic Dust and the spirit and courage that evolves when we learn to give and help others in need.

This is Melissa's first children's book, and as shared in this story, we believe in giving back to our community. Max and the Diaper Fairy supports Diaper Banks across the nation and encourages everyone who receives a visit from The Diaper Fairy to donate your unused diapers to your local Diaper Bank. The Diaper Bank Network ensures that your diapers will be given to those children in need. For more information visit www.maxandthediaperfairy.com.

About The Illustrator

Megan Stringfellow is a freelance artist and illustrator. She and her husband live in Orange County, California.

Megan has been drawing and painting since the she was little, and today creates many different works of art: from handmade stuffed animals and art dolls, to paintings and illustrations. Visit her website at www.stringfellowart.com to see more of her work.

CPSIA information can be obtained
at www.ICGtesting.com
Printed in the USA
BVHW020632070422
633583BV00002B/83